EXPLORING DINOSAURS

APATOSAURUS

By Susan H. Gray

THE CHILD'S WORLD®
CHANHASSEN, MINNESOTA

Published in the United States of America by The Child's World®
P.O. Box 326, Chanhassen, MN 55317-0326
800-599-READ
www.childsworld.com

Content Adviser:
Peter Makovicky,
Ph.D., Curator,
Field Museum,
Chicago, Illinois

Photo Credits: AMNH Photo Studio/American Museum of Natural History Library:
8 (#17507), 16 (#36246); Rick Edwards, Dept. of Paleontology, American Museum
of Natural History Library: 17 bottom; Ben Blackwell & Denis Finnin/American
Museum of Natural History Library: 17 top (#5491), 25 (#5492); Ben Klaffke: 12;
Bettmann/Corbis: 10; Royalty-Free/Corbis: 19; Bill Varie/Corbis: 26–27; Culver
Pictures, Inc.: 18; N. Carter/North Wind Picture Archives: 6; North Wind Picture
Archives: 14; Courtesy of the Peabody Museum of Natural History, Yale University,
New Haven, CT: 15; Jack Fields/Photo Researchers, Inc.: 9; Jean-Philippe Varin/
Jacana/Photo Researchers, Inc.: 11; Francois Gohier/Photo Researchers, Inc.: 13, 22;
Kathy Merrifield/Photo Researchers, Inc.: 23; Ken Lucas/Visuals Unlimited, Inc.: 5,
21; A.J. Copley/Visuals Unlimited, Inc.: 7.

The Child's World®: Mary Berendes, Publishing Director

Editorial Directions, Inc.: E. Russell Primm, Editorial Director; Dana Meachen Rau,
Line Editor; Katie Marsico, Assistant Editor; Matthew Messbarger, Editorial Assistant;
Susan Hindman, Copy Editor; Susan Ashley, Proofreader; Tim Griffin, Indexer; Kerry
Reid, Fact Checker; Dawn Friedman, Photo Reseacher; Linda S. Koutris, Photo Selector

Original cover art by Todd Marshall

The Design Lab: Kathleen Petelinsek, Design and Page Production

Library of Congress Cataloging-in-Publication Data
Gray, Susan Heinrichs.
  Apatosaurus / by Susan H. Gray.
     p. cm. — (Exploring dinosaurs)
Includes index.
Summary: Describes what is known about the physical characteristics, behavior,
habitat, and life cycle of this huge plant-eating dinosaur with the long neck and tail.
  ISBN 1-59296-043-X (lib. bdg. : alk. paper)
  1. Apatosaurus—Juvenile literature. [1. Apatosaurus. 2. Dinosaurs.] I. Title. II. Series.
QE862.S3G692 2004
567.913'8—dc22   2003018630

TABLE OF CONTENTS

R0408293952 JAN · 2007

CHAPTER ONE

AN UNINVITED DINNER GUEST

As the sun was setting, *Apatosaurus* (uh-PAT-oh-SORE-uhss) was still busy with his main task of the day—eating. The dinosaur lumbered forward and swung his enormous neck to the right. He tore a fern from the ground and swallowed it whole. Suddenly, he heard a sound nearby. The *Apatosaurus* looked up just in time. A fierce *Allosaurus* (AL-oh-SORE-uhss) was coming straight toward him.

The *Apatosaurus* whipped his huge tail and knocked over the oncoming dinosaur. The *Allosaurus* never got back up. *Apatosaurus* slowly lowered his head and went back to the ferns.

One hundred and fifty million years later, scientists in North America were looking for fossils. They discovered pieces of a

Apatosaurus *was known for its long neck and its enormous tail, which could be used to injure or kill* enemies. *Although scientists believe* Allosaurus *was more intelligent than* Apatosaurus, *a powerful blow from* Apatosaurus's *tail could make the meat-eater wish it had looked for a meal somewhere else!*

A replica of an Allosaurus *head. During a hunt,* Allosaurus *may have tried to attack an* Apatosaurus *that was already sick or wounded.*

dinosaur skeleton. The pieces looked like they came from an enormous creature. The scientists named it *Apatosaurus,* which means "deceptive lizard." They may have used this name because the bones looked so much like those of other dinosaurs.

CHAPTER TWO

WHAT IS AN APATOSAURUS?

The *Apatosaurus* is a dinosaur that lived about 155 million to 144 million years ago, during the Jurassic (ju-RASS-ik) period. It was one of the largest land animals that ever lived, and grew up to 70 to 80 feet (21 to 24 meters) long. At the end of its long,

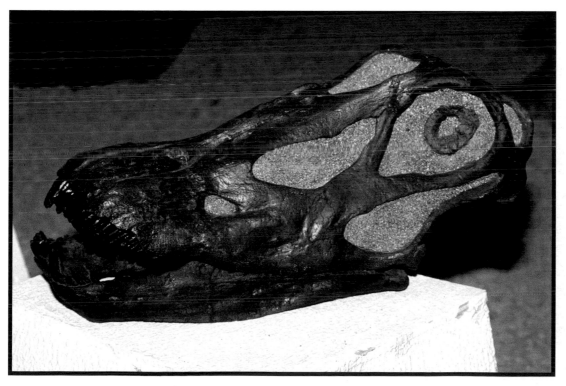

An Apatosaurus *skull. At the end of such an extremely long neck was a head that rarely measured more than 2 feet (0.6 m) long.*

muscular neck was a small head. The dinosaur's brain was about the size of a baseball. Its nostrils sat high on the top of its head, just above and in front of its eyes. Its mouth was filled with teeth shaped like unsharpened pencils.

The fully grown **reptile** could weigh as much as 30 tons. Its body moved around on four massive legs. Big, broad feet that were 2 feet (0.6 m) wide pounded the ground as it walked. The back legs were longer than the front legs, so the dinosaur's back sloped downward

These Apatosaurus *legs were mounted at the American Museum of Natural History in New York. Scientists believe* Apatosaurus *probably moved slowly.*

from the hips to the shoulders. At the hips, *Apatosaurus* was about 15 feet (4.6 m) tall. The animal's mighty tail was up to 30 feet (9 m) long and narrowed down to a long, slender tip.

At one time, scientists believed that the dinosaur must have dragged its immense tail as it walked. *Apatosaurus* trackways tell a different story, however. Trackways are trails of footprints that dinosaurs have left behind. If *Apatosaurus* dragged its tail, then it would have left marks in the trackways. As it turns out, there are no signs at all of tail-dragging. It appears the dinosaur walked along with its tail up in the air.

A museum exhibit displays an Apatosaurus *skeleton, including the extremely long, whiplike tail.* Apatosaurus *fossils such as this one have also been found in Idaho, Wyoming, Utah, and Colorado.*

CHAPTER THREE

WHAT WAS THE JURASSIC PERIOD?

The Jurassic period is the stretch of time from 208 million

years ago to 144 million years ago. During that time, the

earth was very different from the way it is today. The **climate** was

This drawing shows various dinosaurs that existed during the Jurassic period. Although they cannot be seen in this picture, the first birds also appeared during this time. They probably looked more like dinosaurs, however, than the feathered birds we see in our skies today.

much warmer. Many places were covered with short plants and trees. Food for giant, plant-eating dinosaurs grew everywhere.

Apatosaurus wandered the lands now known as North America and Europe. One of its huge, plant-eating relatives, *Diplodocus* (di-PLOD-uh-kuss), also lived in North America

A replica of Diplodocus. *Although mostly covered by water in this picture,* Diplodocus's *tail was similar to that of* Apatosaurus. *Both dinosaurs probably used their strong tails for protection.*

about this time. These two dinosaurs were among the biggest animals ever to exist on Earth. At the end of the Jurassic period, some dinosaurs became **extinct.** These two giants were among them.

CHAPTER FOUR

HOW DO WE KNOW
ABOUT *APATOSAURUS?*

Everything we know about *Apatosaurus*—and about any dinosaur—comes from studying fossils. Fossils are the remains of plants and animals that lived long ago. Dinosaur bones, eggs, and footprints are a few examples of fossils. **Ancient** leaf imprints on rocks are another example. People who study fossils are called paleontologists (PAY-lee-un-TAWL-uh-jists). Paleontologists find fossils

This fossil of a dinosaur footprint can tell scientists quite a lot about the animal and how it lived. Depending on the number and location of footprints, scientists can sometimes determine how fast a dinosaur moved, where it lived, and whether it traveled alone or in a herd.

Fossilized Apatosaurus *bones are on display at the Dinosaur National Monument Quarry in Utah. One of the most complete* Apatosaurus *skeletons ever found was unearthed there in 1909.*

in streambeds, caves, valleys, steep cliffs, and mountainsides.

In the 1870s, two famous paleontologists in America hired

crews to help them look for fossils. The paleontologists were Othniel

Charles Marsh and Edward Drinker Cope. Each man wanted to find

Edward Drinker Cope (shown here) and Othniel Charles Marsh started out as friends. They met in Europe and did some fossil hunting together in the United States before they became enemies.

more dinosaurs than the other. Their crews spied on each other. They stole fossils from each other. They even blew up their own digging places to keep anyone else from looking there. Their **feud** became known as The Great Bone Wars.

In 1877, Marsh's team discovered a few bones. Right away, Marsh described the dinosaur to all of his scientist friends. He gave it the name *Apatosaurus*. Shortly after that, his crew found bones from another dinosaur. Marsh, still wanting to outdo Cope,

This photograph shows one of Marsh's fossil-hunting expeditions. Most of Marsh's finds as a fossil hunter are either at the Peabody Museum in New Haven, Connecticut, or at the Smithsonian Institution in Washington, D.C. Cope's discoveries are housed at the Academy of Natural Sciences in Philadelphia, Pennsylvania.

claimed it was a whole new dinosaur—*Brontosaurus*. In 1903, a third paleontologist, Elmer Riggs, showed that the two were really the same dinosaur. Because *Apatosaurus* was the first name used, that is the correct name.

Despite all their battles, the two crews did find many fossils. In fact, Marsh and Cope wrote about more than 130 new dinosaurs from North America. One of these was *Apatosaurus*.

THE DINOSAUR THAT LOST ITS HEAD

About a century ago, paleontologists found a skeleton of *Apatosaurus* that had one big problem. Its skull was missing. Not far away, they found a skull that seemed to fit nicely at the end of the *Apatosaurus*'s neck. However, some people thought the skull was much too small for this huge dinosaur. They thought its little mouth and peglike teeth could never have fed such an animal. Scientists brought the skeleton to the Carnegie Museum in Pittsburgh, Pennsylvania, and rebuilt it. But because the skull seemed too small, they just left it off. The little skull was stored away. For years, people visited the dinosaur with no head.

Then one scientist decided he had found the perfect skull to match the skeleton. It was a big skull, with large, strong teeth. He mounted a model of it on the skeleton and everything seemed fine. Museum visitors were pleased to see that the dinosaur finally had a head.

Years and years passed. Then an expert came and took a look at things. He examined all kinds of *Apatosaurus* bones. He read notes that workers had written as they dug up the bones. He decided the skeleton was wearing the wrong skull. The big skull was not the right one at all! The museum finally agreed. They held a special ceremony where they took off the big skull and mounted the little one that had been stored away. At last, everyone thought, *Apatosaurus* had the right head.

CHAPTER FIVE

HOW HIGH COULD THE DINOSAUR LIFT ITS HEAD?

For years, people believed that *Apatosaurus* could gaze over the treetops. Artists painted pictures of the dinosaur plucking its food from high branches. Museum skeletons held their heads up in

This painting shows an Apatosaurus *holding its head high in the air. Scientists—and artists—once imagined that* Apatosaurus *and its relatives grazed on high tree leaves like giraffes do.*

This replica of an Apatosaurus *is more realistic in showing how high the dinosaur could lift its head. Scientists also believe the type of plants that stretched high up during the Jurassic period wouldn't have provided enough food for such an enormous dinosaur.*

the air. Everyone thought *Apatosaurus* could lift its head high above the ground.

Now many scientists are taking a different view. They believe the dinosaur could not lift its head more than 15 to 20 feet (4.6 to

6.1 m) off the ground. There are two reasons for this. First, the

bones in its neck would not allow it. If the dinosaur tried to raise its

head very high, its neck bones would bump into each other as the

neck bent. The neck would not be able to bend very far at all.

The second reason has to do with the dinosaur's heart. As

Apatosaurus lifted its head higher and higher, its heart would have

had to pump harder and harder to get blood up to it. If the

dinosaur held its head up all the way, its heart would need to

pump blood 20 to 25 feet (6.1 to 7.6 m) straight up. Otherwise,

the dinosaur would pass out! A heart big enough to do that would

have almost filled the dinosaur's chest. There would have been no

room for lungs or anything else. Now scientists think that

Apatosaurus held its head straight out.

CHAPTER SIX

WHAT DID
APATOSAURUS EAT?

Experts believe that the *Apatosaurus* might have found its food on the ground. Perhaps it even ate from low tree branches. It could have swung its huge neck from left to right, eating everything

During the Jurassic period, the Earth was warm and moist. Apatosaurus *probably feasted on plants and trees that thrived in that environment.*

THE OLD GRIND

Paleontologists often find some interesting stones with *Apatosaurus* skeletons. The stones are smooth and rounded. They lie within the dinosaur's rib cage or somewhere nearby. Scientists call them gastroliths (GAS-troh-liths). The stones helped the dinosaur digest its food.

Throughout its life, an *Apatosaurus* would sometimes swallow rocks. Inside, they tossed about as the dinosaur's stomach muscles moved. This helped mash the food into smaller and smaller pieces.

Over time, this movement and the dinosaur's stomach acid would wear the rocks down. That is why gastroliths are so round and smooth.

around it. By standing in one place, and just moving its neck, the dinosaur would have saved lots of energy.

Apatosaurus was an herbivore (UR-buh-vore). This means it only ate plants. It probably pulled up ferns, club mosses, and **horsetails** from the ground. The animal also may have eaten needles and cones from pine trees and the soft leaves of gingko trees.

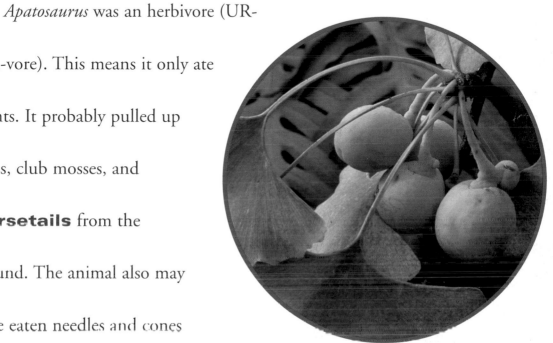

These gingko leaves would have been a tasty meal for Apatosaurus! *Some paleontologists believe that* Apatosaurus *had thick, mooselike lips. These lips would have been useful in gathering leaves such as those shown here.*

The dinosaur's teeth were not good for chewing. So the dinosaur swallowed its food whole. Its huge stomach ground up the plants with the help of stones called gastroliths.

CHAPTER SEVEN

GROWING UP AND GROWING OLD

There was more to life for *Apatosaurus* than just eating all day. The dinosaur had enemies, too. One of the worst was the *Allosaurus. Allosaurus* was a meat eater with powerful jaws and sharp teeth. Scientists believe that it sometimes ate the big plant eaters. They have found *Apatosaurus* bones scarred with *Allosaurus* teeth marks.

Apatosaurus reached an enormous size fairly quickly. Experts believe that it probably took only 12 years for the dinosaur to reach its 30-ton weight. Such quick growth helped the dinosaur survive. The faster it reached its full size, the less likely it was to become **prey.**

Paleontologists can learn plenty by looking at a dinosaur's skele-

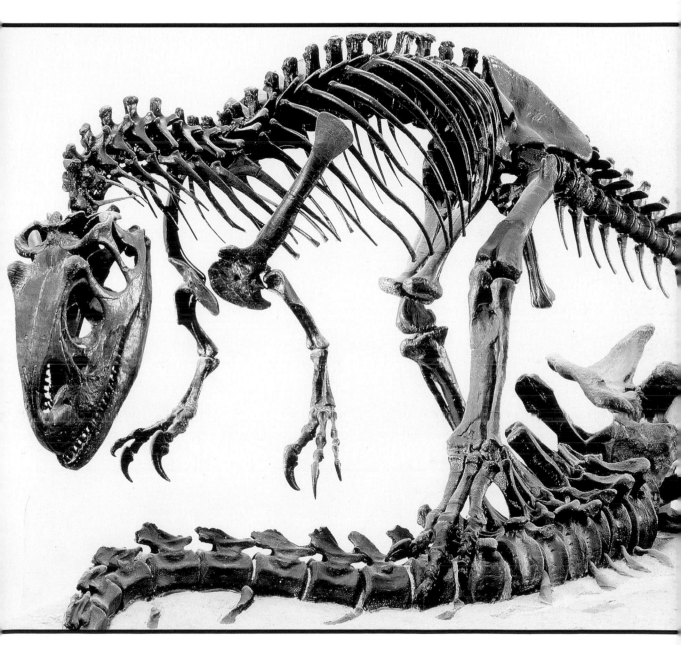

This skeleton of the ferocious Allosaurus *has been set up to show it feeding on the skeleton of an* Apatosaurus. *Though* Allosaurus *was smaller than* Apatosaurus, *it was quicker and had razor-sharp teeth that measured 2 to 4 inches (5 to 10 centimeters).*

Dinosaur skeletons at the Natural History Museum in London, England. The dinosaur with the horns is Triceratops. *This creature lived in the Cretaceous period, which followed the Jurassic period. Like* Apatosaurus, Triceratops *was also an herbivore.*

ton. When they see skull bones grown together, they know that the dinosaur became an adult. When they see teeth that are very worn down, they know the dinosaur made it to old age. Clues from *Apatosaurus* bones show that some of these dinosaurs may have lived to be 100 years old!

Scientists will be studying this mighty creature for years to come. They want to know why it became extinct. They wonder just how big the dinosaur's heart was. And they hope to learn how a baby *Apatosaurus* could grow so quickly. Maybe someday you will help solve some of these mysteries.

Glossary

ancient (AYN-shunt) Something that is ancient is very old; from millions of years ago. An ancient leaf imprint is an example of a fossil.

climate (KLYE-mit) The climate of a place is the usual weather in that place. During the Jurassic period, Earth had a warm climate.

extinct (ek-STINGKT) Something that is extinct no longer exists. Scientists have several ideas about how the dinosaurs may have become extinct.

feud (FYOOD) A feud is a long-lasting argument or quarrel. The Great Bone Wars was a famous feud between paleontologists.

horsetails (HORSS-taylz) Horsetails were ancient sticklike plants. *Apatosaurus* fed on horsetails.

prey (PRAY) Prey are animals that are eaten by other animals. *Apatosaurus* was less likely to become prey for other dinosaurs once it reached its full size.

reptile (REP-tile) A reptile is an air-breathing animal with a backbone and is usually covered with scales or plates. *Apatosaurus* was a reptile.

Did You Know?

▶ When paleontologist Elmer Riggs found a huge *Apatosaurus* skeleton in Colorado, newspapers all over the world went wild. One even showed a picture of *Apatosaurus* walking down a street in Chicago!

▶ A wealthy man named Andrew Carnegie hired people to search for dinosaur skeletons. One of them found a new type of *Apatosaurus*. The new dinosaur was named *Apatosaurus louisae,* in honor of Carnegie's wife, Louise.

▶ Although *Apatosaurus* is the dinosaur's correct name, most people still know the animal by its old, incorrect name, *Brontosaurus*.

The Geologic Time Scale

TRIASSIC PERIOD

Date: 248 million to 208 million years ago

Fossils: *Coelophysis, Cynodont, Desmatosuchus, Eoraptor, Gerrothorax, Peteinosaurus, Placerias, Plateosaurus, Postosuchus, Procompsognathus, Riojasaurus, Saltopus, Teratosaurus, Thecodontosaurus*

Distinguishing Features: For the most part, the climate in the Triassic period was hot and dry. The first true mammals appeared during this period, as well as turtles, frogs, salamanders, and lizards. Corals could also be found in oceans at this time, although large reefs such as the ones we have today did not yet exist. Evergreen trees made up much of the plant life.

JURASSIC PERIOD

Date: 208 million to 144 million years ago

Fossils: *Allosaurus, Anchisaurus, Apatosaurus, Barosaurus, Brachiosaurus, Ceratosaurus, Compsognathus, Cryptoclidus, Dilophosaurus, Diplodocus, Eustreptospondylus, Hybodus, Janenschia, Kentrosaurus, Liopleurodon, Megalosaurus, Opthalmosaurus, Rhamphorhynchus, Saurolophus, Segisaurus, Seismosaurus, Stegosaurus, Supersaurus, Syntarsus, Ultrasaurus, Vulcanodon, Xiaosaurus*

Distinguishing Features: The climate of the Jurassic period was warm and moist. The first birds appeared during this period. Plant life was also greener and more widespread. Sharks began swimming in Earth's oceans. Although dinosaurs didn't even exist at the beginning of the Triassic period, they ruled Earth by Jurassic times. There was a minor mass extinction toward the end of the Jurassic period.

CRETACEOUS PERIOD

Date: 144 million to 65 million years ago

Fossils: *Acrocanthosaurus, Alamosaurus, Albertosaurus, Anatotitan, Ankylosaurus, Argentinosaurus, Bagaceratops, Baryonyx, Carcharodontosaurus, Carnotaurus, Centrosaurus, Chasmosaurus, Corythosaurus, Didelphodon, Edmontonia, Edmontosaurus, Gallimimus, Gigantosaurus, Hadrosaurus, Hypsilophodon, Iguanodon, Kronosaurus, Lambeosaurus, Leaellynasaura, Maiasaura, Megaraptor, Muttaburrasaurus, Nodosaurus, Ornithocheirus, Oviraptor, Pachycephalosaurus, Panoplosaurus, Parasaurolophus, Pentaceratops, Polacanthus, Protoceratops, Psittacosaurus, Quaesitosaurus, Saltasaurus, Sarcosuchus, Saurolophus, Sauropelta, Saurornithoides, Segnosaurus, Spinosaurus, Stegoceras, Stygimoloch, Styracosaurus, Tapejara, Tarbosaurus, Therizinosaurus, Thescelosaurus, Torosaurus, Trachodon, Triceratops, Troodon, Tyrannosaurus rex, Utahraptor, Velociraptor*

Distinguishing Features: The climate of the Cretaceous period was fairly mild. Flowering plants first appeared in this period, and many modern plants developed. With flowering plants came a greater diversity of insect life. Birds further developed into two types: flying and flightless. A wider variety of mammals also existed. At the end of this period came a great mass extinction that wiped out the dinosaurs, along with several other groups of animals.

How to Learn More

At the Library

Lambert, David, Darren Naish, and Liz Wyse. *Dinosaur Encyclopedia.*
New York: DK Publishing, 2001.

Landau, Elaine. *Apatosaurus.*
Danbury, Conn.: Children's Press, 1999.

On the Web

Visit our home page for lots of links about *Apatosaurus:*
http://www.childsworld.com/links.html
Note to Parents, Teachers, and Librarians: We routinely verify our
Web links to make sure they're safe, active sites—so encourage
your readers to check them out!

Places to Visit or Contact

AMERICAN MUSEUM OF NATURAL HISTORY
To view numerous dinosaur fossils, as well
as the fossils of several ancient mammals
Central Park West at 79th Street
New York, NY 10024-5192
212/769-5100

CARNEGIE MUSEUM OF NATURAL HISTORY
To see an Apatosaurus *skeleton*
4400 Forbes Avenue
Pittsburgh, PA 15213
412/622-3131

DINOSAUR NATIONAL MONUMENT
To view a huge deposit of dinosaur bones in a natural setting
4545 East Highway 40
Dinosaur, CO 81610-9724
or
DINOSAUR NATIONAL MONUMENT
(QUARRY)
11625 East 1500 South
Jensen, UT 84035
435/781-7700

MUSEUM OF THE ROCKIES
To see real dinosaur fossils, as well as robotic replicas
Montana State University
600 West Kagy Boulevard
Bozeman, MT 59717-2730
406/994-2251 or 406/994-DINO (3466)

NATIONAL MUSEUM OF NATURAL HISTORY
(SMITHSONIAN INSTITUTION)
To see several dinosaur exhibits and special behind-the-scenes tours
10th Street and Constitution Avenue, N.W.
Washington, DC 20560-0166
202/357-2700

Index

About the Author

Susan H. Gray has bachelor's and master's degrees in zoology, and has taught college-level courses in biology. She first fell in love with fossil hunting while studying paleontology in college. In her 25 years as an author, she has written many articles for scientists and researchers, and many science books for children. Susan enjoys gardening, traveling, and playing the piano. She and her husband, Michael, live in Cabot, Arkansas.